CAVESHA FOX NERO

Reviving Womanhood

Take Me To The Water

To the women who strive each day to live their true and full lives, in love and service to their families and communities. You persevere and leave legacies of inspiration and hope for future generations to aspire to.

Contents

Preface	ii
1 The Origin	1
2 Generational Culture Changes	7
3 The Stain of Modern Culture	13
4 Return of the Basics: Ode to Foundations	28
5 Social Advantage of the Shift	37
About the Author	50
Also by Cavesha Fox Nero	51

Preface

Is the concept of being a lady lost in modern culture? Is it possible to meet a woman who has not been swayed by mainstream trends and extreme antithetical belief systems? These are questions posed in conversation surrounding the present state of womanhood. A discussion of historical timelines where the culture of women shifted, will be addressed. Compared to other nations, present day America recognizes the importance of women and the influence they hold. Having knowledge of this should urge the seasoned (wise) women to rise, putting up a strategic resistance to the negative influence and rhetoric targeted to infiltrate families, mentally poisoning women as early as girlhood. Women are extraordinarily created with a myriad of values, gifts, and talents. These attributes should not be tarnished, exchanged, or discarded, simply because women are capable of expansion, stepping into roles that their aspirations, or the hardships of life, may transition them into.

Mature and resolute women across the world desire to be needed and feel accomplished. They daily seek out ways to fulfill their purpose by being a necessary support figure. It is critical to recognize the women who demonstrate upstanding character rather than fleeting trends. This book encourages evaluation of the messages delivered to women. The reader will be able to determine if popular messages are helping or harming the overall female image. Topics addressed include historical references, marriage, destructive cultures, manipulative media messaging, and the feminist movement. This analysis ultimately explores the uniqueness of womanhood, and the ill willed, preconceived notions against women's distinction and significance.

1

The Origin

It is of a truth that various people presume knowledge of who a woman is, along with her functions that contribute to the overall grandeur of creation. As many women develop and experience adolescence, college, the dating world, marriage, and children, there will be much more to add to the list of initial beliefs. In research of the actual definition of the term "woman", it presents that a woman is an adult female human being. The term "lady" is described as a polite or old-fashioned reference of a girl or woman, akin to a gentlewoman. Being called a lady is viewed as more of a formal, respectful address for a woman.

Creation View and Biblical Mentions

For those who are of faith base or spiritual inclination, observing a woman's significance is not arduous. Most devout raised Christian women are taught their value and worth as a child. God's plan for the female's creation was masterly, lacking no error. The book of Genesis states that God created the first man, Adam, and gave him a job for a basis of responsibility, stability, and dominion. Evidently Adam tended the garden of Eden well. He even named the animals that God formed. After all of this, Adam was still viewed by our Creator as being "alone".

God then created the first woman, Eve (from Adam), to be his "helpmate". The animals were not considered comparable to Adam for fulfillment of this specific role.

The premise was established that a woman was to be an assister to the man and vision accomplishment. With her rendering help, she was in exchange to be "covered". It is important to note that God would not have created Eve for Adam if Adam was not qualified or deserving of her. This was ascertained from how he managed his daily responsibilities. Adam was actively managing and providing in the garden "before" Eve's creation. The term "covering" is described as a protective mechanism against exposure to enemies and potential harm. The man's role was to protect and pour into who assisted him. What a powerful and wise establishment. Our Creator's plan far outwitted any human knowledge. Before the fall of Adam and Eve, God knew that the man and woman would always need one another.

When looking at what determines the values of a woman, there are numerous scriptural descriptions of the attributes a woman should possess. These qualities create value of her life and in the lives of those around her. A renowned reference is found in the book of Proverbs, chapter 31. The passage expounds on the characteristics of a noble wife. A woman with the presented qualities of being present, loving, wise, kind, selfless, hardworking, resourceful, and respectful, was highly coveted. This type of "virtuous" woman brought honor to herself, her husband, and her household. She awakened earlier to ensure that her husband, children, and the household helpers were fed and had everything they needed for the day. This type of woman was able to operate in her feminine characteristics because she had a traditional husband who fulfilled his roles. He had to have exhibited love, provision, and protection. Once her household responsibilities were taken care of, she was then able to do work outside of the home for additional income. This was simply an asset to the provision already in place. She was also referenced to be wise with finances in that she considered property and purchased the land. Her husband viewed her as trustworthy, praising her conduct. Traditional-leaning Christian churches still embrace this scriptural reference as a basis for characteristics that produce excellent results in women's lives.

Esther was a great biblical example of a woman using her new-found status as queen, to be of service to her people. Esther was a virgin, Jewish young lady who went through a twelve-month purification period to become queen to King Xerxes of Persia. The rituals of beauty treatments were stringent, inclusive of six months of applying oil of myrrh and six months of perfumes and cosmetics, preparing for the time to present before the king. In the book of Esther, chapter 7, Esther faced a life altering choice. She could deny the plight of her people's suffering, choosing to enjoy her new rank in the king's palace, or risk death by displeasing the king to be true to her character of meeting the need of her people. She found favor in the king's site and humbly requested that the persecution end. By her displaying grace and a disposition of compassion, it caused the king to spare Mordecai's (her cousin and guardian) life, and the lives of the Jewish people. Promotion transpired in Esther and Mordecai's life because Esther was "in position and selfless". Good women must possess good works and a genuine concern for the livelihood of those who, to some, may not appear to be on their status level.

Another exemplary woman deserving of mention is Hannah. Hannah was a wife to Elkanah. They lived in Ephraim. The first chapter of the first book of Samuel notedly mentions how Hannah was still loved by her husband, even though she suffered with barrenness. Peninnah, Elkanah's other wife, would cruelly taunt Hannah for not having children. When it was time to make annual sacrifices in Shiloh, Elkanah gave a double portion to Hannah. This gesture displayed that he showed love, kindness, and concern for Hannah, who had grown weary and ceased eating from her distress. Her sadness and anxiety worried Elkanah. Hannah prayed fervently in the temple and the priest, Eli, saw her. He prayed that God would grant her petition for a male child that she promised to wean and dedicate back to the Lord's service. God remembered Hannah's prayers and her faith. She conceived and birthed Samuel. When the time came, Samuel was taken to be trained by Eli, the priest. Samuel became a powerfully anointed prophet and judge in Israel. He installed and advised King Saul. He also anointed David as a young man. David would be the future successor of King Saul. By Hannah praying earnestly, she experienced the miraculous move of God. She honorably kept her word and unselfishly allowed her gift (Samuel) to be shared, for the good of the people. Wherein a mother's love could have shielded her son, she released him to "purpose", giving him back to the will of "the Giver".

A final biblical woman to reference is Ruth. Ruth was from Moab (in the modern state of Jordan). She married a Judean immigrant. After about ten years, Ruth's husband died, along with his brother. This forced Ruth to decide if she would return to her native land, now being a widow without child. Ruth's mother-in-law, Naomi, was a widow and facing life without her sons. She was alone deciding to make the journey back to Bethlehem. Amid Ruth's angst, she ignored Naomi's request for her to return to her premarital home. Ruth decided to take it upon herself to follow Naomi and care for her. Ruth's unselfish decision presented kindness, gratitude, and respect for the years of Naomi being her mother-in-law and for the fact that Naomi was an elder. Ruth went to Bethlehem and found work as a gleaner in the fields. This points to another area of value being in women's ability to "shift gears". Ruth taking on a harder lifestyle as a single widow, was praiseworthy. She was a determined woman, honoring her elder, Naomi, by standing in the gap as her "help". Ruth's behaviors captured the attention and favor of Boaz, a rich and prominent man. He went as far as to inquire of her (Side note: Do our mannerisms and behaviors summon inquiries of us from possible marital mates?). Boaz was in the lineage of Jesus Christ. He became a "kinsman redeemer" acting as a foreshadowing of Christ's sacrifice for mankind, as Jesus was the ultimate Redeemer. Boaz married Ruth and she conceived a son, securing Ruth and Naomi's future livelihood.

Historical Timeline Review-Before Feminism

Starting with where most records can be traced, the Middle (Dark) Ages (476 AD - 1450 AD), books, articles, television shows, and movies depict women of this era in various ways. In most of the world at the time, a woman was often either wealthy or poor. Most women who worked outside of the home were doing so to help their household financial status. Working-class women in the Middle Ages cooked, were spinners, helped run farms, and hauled well water and firewood. Eventually, European countries developed what is known as a "middle class" composed of business owners, some of which were women. In the early Middle Ages, a woman's religion determined much of what her roles could be, in comparison with the secular or pagan society where a woman's abilities were largely attached to her social class (who she married, family history, and financial standing).

Christianity was spreading and it was allowing women of any social class to hold positions of power. St. Hilda of Whitby (614 AD- 680 AD) was recorded as being a virgin woman who dedicated her life to founding and serving as an abbess of a monastery in Whitby of North Yorkshire, England. She was reported to demonstrate energy, skilled administrative and teaching abilities, and a mother-like spirit to all, specifically those considered "common folk". Muslim women in elite households were often educated, but not permitted to participate in official legal bodies. These Muslim women were allowed to study and teach on subjects among other women. Some sources reveal that

Muslim women were allowed to manage independent wealth, conduct investments, trade, and initiate divorce.

The role and view of women from the 1600s into the 1700s also hinged on social class. In general, women were not allowed to be teachers, doctors, or lawyers in profession. Women were mainly homemakers, tailoresses, embroiderers, milliners, brewers, or bakers. What noticeably made women unique in this time frame was the multi-tasking. Affluent women were afforded the privilege of hired servants to complete the numerous tasks that helped manage the home and estate; however, lower economic class women, bore the load of these tasks. There were no vacuum cleaners, automatic dish washers, washing machines, cars, or easy methods to complete regular chores. Clothes washing or dyeing was by hand. A farmer's wife, for example, would have to feed animals, grow fruits and vegetables, cure meat, cook, and still ensure her husband and children had all of their needs met. A woman also continued to be a nurse for her family. Only wealthy women could afford a household physician. The type and duration of education in this time frame was contingent on the woman's economic class. A merchant's daughter was likely to learn how to run a business, especially if he had no sons. Middle-class girls were taught reading, writing, arithmetic, and sewing.

Towards the late 18th century, there were noted educational and occupational changes, as few women pursued studies in astronomy, physics, and mathematics. A famous Italian mathematician was Maria Agnesi (1718-1799). She was multilingual and known for her significant contributions to differential calculus. Agnesi was cited as the first woman to write a mathematics handbook. In 1828, at 77 years old, Caroline Herschel (1750-1848) of Hanover, Germany, was awarded the Gold Medal of the Royal Astronomical Society. She remarkably contributed to astronomy by way of discovering numerous comets.

2

Generational Culture Changes

First Wave Feminism (1848-1920)

Feminism is defined as an ideology that women should not be regulated to domesticated tasks, subjected by their husbands, or treated as second-class citizens. Women in this time period organized privately and eventually publicly, displaying activism efforts to change laws in hopes of expanding the rights of women in the United States. In 1848, the first women's rights convention was held in Seneca Falls, New York addressing the civil, social, and religious state of women. The goals of first wave feminism appeared innocent. Without recognition, women were often beacons and constructive influences behind the scenes in their families and communities. It is of popular opinion that women should have always been afforded the right to have equal say, representation, and own property. First wave feminism contributed positively in raising awareness of domestic violence, specifically as a result of male alcohol abuse. They advocated for the prohibition of alcohol through a temperance movement. In 1874, a group of these women founded the Women's Christian Temperance Union (WCTU) due to their argument of alcohol causing men to physically assault their wives.

The first wave female abolitionists received insurmountable pushback for speaking publicly against slavery. These feminists fought for all women, outside of social status, to have a right to university level education. By 1837, Oberlin University, in the state of Ohio, became the first college to allow women's enrollment for bachelor's degrees. In 1890, to secure the right to vote for women in the United States, the National American Woman Suffrage Association (NAWSA) was formed from the merging of the Democratic and Republican suffrage organizations. There arose more opposition, referred to as "Petticoat Rule", where anti-feminists believed and asserted that the progressive move of women's rights would change society negatively, causing women to rule over and oppress the men. Hunger strikes, marches, and other demonstrations, led to President Woodrow Wilson supporting the Nineteenth Amendment to the United States Constitution in 1920. Susan B. Anthony, Elizabeth Cady Stanton, Ida B. Wells, and Frances Willard were prominent in the progression of this first feminist movement. While this first wave of feminism was taking place in America, across other countries such as the Netherlands, Germany, France, Canada, and South Korea, they were also experiencing an increase in efforts to provide or expand on women's rights through demonstrations, conventions, and joining of various feminist groups.

By the early 19th century, the institution of marriage also underwent changes. Women begin marrying later, at an average age of 22 years old. Women's roles in rural areas was still found to be more traditional, in comparison to women living in or near cities. Rural dwelling women were more likely to remain homemakers, birthing higher numbers of children, and managing numerous household responsibilities. World War I (1914-1918) and the Industrial Revolution (1876-1900) required large volumes of workers to produce goods at a fast pace. There were not enough men to meet this demand, especially in the United States, at the time. This launched women into the workforce to fill manufacturing, agricultural, and healthcare positions due to the millions of men engaged in battle.

In late 1945, post-World War II, American women in the workforce were expected to return back to their homes to carry out feminine, traditional roles and functions again. Many of these women did, fostering the surge of advertising for the image of the 1950s housewife. Complaints from critics of women's post war return, noted that the age of marriage saw a decrease to age 20 for women. By the 1950s, about 60 percent of enrolled female college students dropped out of college to get married or to become more desirable by men for marriage.

Second Wave Feminism (*1960s- 1980s*)

A popular book titled *The Second Sex,* was authored by French feminist, Simone de Beauvoir in 1949. The author addressed womanhood and the historical treatment of women as subjugated by men. Ms. de Beauvoir posited that a woman is not born but that she becomes a woman. Ideas and philosophies such as this grew. In 1963 Betty Friedan authored *The Feminine Mystique,* a book detailing interviews and resources from women of how being a housewife and child rearing did not provide a sense of purpose. Friedan believed that the feminine mystique seemed to deny women a basic right to growth, further relaying that women would rather remain unhappy in their traditional roles where children would grow up with unfulfilled mothers.

The rise of certain "women going their own way (WGTOW today)", propelled the Second wave feminist movement in America and other western countries. These feminists mainly focused on addressing and solving public and private injustices against women. Reproductive rights, assault, domestic violence, and workplace safety were at the forefront of this movement. Middle class white women were large promoters of this wave. The late 1960s to 1970s showed a decreased desire to form any identity from being a wife and mother. There was an increased desire to pursue "perceived" happiness and wholeness in individuality.

In 1961, the U.S. Food and Drug Administration (FDA) approved oral contraceptive pills. The usage of these pills increased by the 1970s in other developed countries. A June 14, 2006 report from Oxford Academic relayed that, as of 1975, American women had 2.0 children. Roe v. Wade ruled that the U.S. Constitution protected a pregnant individual's liberty to have an abortion. On June 10, 1963, President John F. Kennedy signed the Equal Pay Act of 1963, abolishing wage disparity based on sex. Title VII of the Civil Rights Act of 1964 was amended to protect employees and job applicants from employment discrimination based on race, color, religion, sex, and national origin. Another highlight was the Pregnancy Discrimination Act of 1978 that made employer discrimination illegal against pregnant employees. Furthermore, in 1986 the legislation of no-fault divorce was established. In previous years, a couple would have to state the specific reasons for divorce. They also would need to have been separated for a certain amount of time before an official divorce.

Third Wave Feminism (*1990s-2012*)

In the mid-1990s, Generation X women ushered in third wave feminism. The purpose of this movement was stated to further support and create more groups working towards gender, economic, racial, and social justice. Third wave feminists sought to question, reclaim, and redefine the words, ideas, and media that transmitted ideas pertaining to womanhood, gender, beauty, sexuality, femininity, and masculinity. Perceptions of gender deteriorated. The notions of certain characteristics being strictly male, and others being solely female, were considered defunct. They supported the position of sexual liberation and free love from the second wave, incorporating gender fluidity assertions of sex as well. Minority women were heavily grafted into this movement. These minority female professionals continued to increase in corporate America, and they filled many other prominent positions outside of the home.

Portrayals of women in music, television shows, and movies, intensified in sensual nature, elevating the display of women being underdressed, emotionally unstable, and involved in revolving purposeless sexual relationships. Television shows such as "Sex in the City" and "Girlfriends", displayed career-driven character versions of women in their late twenties and thirties, only coveting marriage and motherhood as an "end of the road, once tired" choice. The topic of marriage and children was not as significant in a woman's life, nor on par with her functions outside of the home. Creating and maintaining a family was perceived as a distraction from (or obstruction to) personal career growth.

Fourth Wave Feminism (2012- present)

There are modern women who still believe they are "starting from ground zero" as it pertains to female rights. The fourth wave emerged from a new generation of women who, by large, had not been well informed of previous waves through their education at high school, institutions, and universities. The internet and media outlets produced massive traction for this movement. As of now, fourth wave feminism exists to continue awareness of stated issues to include sexual harassment, abuse, sexism, and objectification in the workplace. The wave also expanded to focus more on marginalized communities to include LGBTQIA+ people's rights. Critics posit that fourth wave feminists are abreast of and promoters of the latest "pronoun" etiquette regime. These latter wave feminists believe that biological males can become women and that there are no distinctions between a biological female, or one who has transitioned. Research shows that the aim of fourth wave feminists is to continue advocating for increased societal participation,

11

power, and equal pay.

The "Me Too Movement" originated in 2017 in the United States and begin to spread in other western and eastern countries. The aim of the movement was to empower alleged victims of sexual abuse and sexual harassment. Known American female actors and other celebrities began to publicly voice and allege that they were victims of sexual misconduct. Social media is a large catalyst for fourth wave feminism. It is a line of communication that quickly travels. Social media allows women to share their alleged or proven experiences from all over the world, providing a space where they can be heard, receive validation, and rally for change. In previous feminist movements, conferences and meetings were mainly at brick-and-mortar locations. With this movement, meetups were also arranged and conducted online with greater group organization strength. By some, fourth wave feminism is considered to be an enhanced continuation of third wave feminism.

A 2016 Child Trends study showed that 40 percent of births in the United States occurred outside of marriage, an increase from 28 percent in 1990. Women in the fourth wave movement who did choose to have children, were choosing to do so outside of the nuclear family structure. Common law marriages were widespread as well. A February 26, 2020 article from the Center for Equal Opportunity documented that 39.6 percent of American births in 2018 were outside of marriage. An alarming concern was that, nonmarital births broken down among ethnic groups, presented as 69.4 percent African American, 51.8 percent Hispanic, 28.2 percent white, and 11.7 percent Asian American.

3

The Stain of Modern Culture

Although there were notable rights granted to women, there persists a divide between western women across age groups on who a woman is and what her roles and functions are. This rive is evident by what these women believe concerning womanhood and the communication blocks between, for example, a Baby Boomer and a Generation Z woman. The traced American generations are composed of the Silent Generation (born 1928-1945), Baby Boomers (born 1946-1964), Generation X (born 1965-1980), Millennials (born 1981-1996), and Generation Z (born 1997-2010). A Silent Generation woman embodied completely different values and opinions of ladyhood than a Generation X or Millennial woman. Concerning the subject of marriage and children, most Silent Generation females were married by the age of 20, birthing more children. In contrast, a modern Generation Z woman is more apt to look at marriage and motherhood as a "last to-do" on the checklist, if desired at all. In 2022, research showed that the average age of marriage for females was 30 years old.

Did feminist forerunners have wins and losses, based on how women are viewed and treated today? Did they inadvertently set future generations of women up for regressions amid some progressions?

Since second wave feminism, a grave issue of concern is that women (outside of principled family units or religious groups), see no purpose for abstinence. In previous generations, a vital part of a woman's value was one of her wrapped gifts (virginity). This was not to imply that it was the sole thing giving women value, however, it was an important and esteemed component of women and pursuant men. A lady in waiting had to be convinced that a pursuing man was "worth" marrying, then upon marriage, sharing her body with, and carrying children for. The moral woman's bar of expectation was set high, further postulating that a man must present himself with possessed values and qualities in order to even have the time and attention of that woman.

The effect of the different waves of feminism in the United States imprinted broader society in ways that were not all positive, nor constructive to a healthy and wholesome social culture. Modern males and females are not waiting, nor are they encouraged to wait until the age of 18 to engage in sexual activity and procreation. Many are familiar with the known phrase "protect our girls". Liberal society members should back off when proactive fathers and mothers instill morals, standards, and boundaries for their teens lives as protective measures. Fathers should not be publicly vilified by feminist platforms, as has been done, for putting barriers in place to shield their minor aged daughters from all potential sexual harm, including consensual sex participation. If a teenager is still a child, a child must be directed. The same feminist accusers of fathers being too strict or rules oriented will cast stones and judgment if their female teen is kidnapped, becomes pregnant, or is revealed to be involved in a secret domestic violence relationship under the father's nose.

Support and vocalized advocacy should also be given for the protection of teens mental and emotional well-being from other dangerous sources. An observed issue is that there does not seem to be enough accommodations given to female adolescents to ensure that they are protected on all fronts, including protection from those in their own age group. Efforts of protection must be executed to prevent the entrapment of negative cultures. This includes vetting and getting to know a young lady's friends, their friends' parents, coaches, teachers, the social media influencers they follow, and other entertainment mediums they gravitate to (encompassing the music they listen to). These things affect the adolescent's overall behavior. Their minds are being molded from encounters and experiences. Parents should be the first teachers to their children and the gentle force throughout their lives.

In modern culture, it is common for female teens to, with parental approval or without it, leave the home and go places well after dark with males for one-on-one dates that could lead to unwanted outcomes if these teens have not been trained well, or if they choose to go against what they have been taught, to "experiment". Regular viral social media posts and pictures showcase female teenagers doing very "adult like" things, overnight trips with boyfriends and parents renting hotel rooms for the "minors" to have prom night after-parties. Even the modern "Sweet 16" celebrations of today are totally different than those in times past. These are parties that refer to female teens as crossing over into young adulthood. The celebrations now appear to be no more than glam parties versus a presentation of a matured and developed young lady, accountable for her own actions. The average westernized young lady, with the exception of those from traditional backgrounds, is sadly not even trained by 16 years of age on proper adornment, hygiene, cooking, cleaning, decorating, manners and etiquette, appropriate and respectful communication, or money management. If these trainings are unnecessary for teenagers because they are "still children", why allow children to participate in so many adult activities (including consensual sex) without the responsibilities that accompany such behaviors? Even children must be instructed. We are to train up a child in the way they "should" go. It is not to say they will not stray, but the truth of the better way must be instilled in them.

Referencing the Victorian Era (1837-1901), 16 to 21 year old females were considered biologically mature and skills trained (by active parents' arrangement of these years- long preparation services), demonstrating that they had "come of age" and were ready for public display. They attended galas or balls being introduced as young "ladies" readying or ready for a suitor in attendance seeking courtship and a wife. There are still middle and upper class American families active with various social groups such as Jack and Jill of America. Debutante balls are also continually held, formally debuting cotillion-trained young ladies to society. The origin of families presenting their daughters at these events as "ready to court and marry" in former Europe and America, has since revised. The purpose is now stated to serve as a healthy, formal social event for teenagers, community outreach, and charity.

If something is not broken, why does it need to be fixed? Through false proclamations of female sexual empowerment, the sexual revolution of the 1960s to present, hurts women by lying to them. The movement provided "men" with a key of access to what they may not qualify for. To women's present day detriment, they have been taught to believe that love should not possess a business aspect or appear transactional in any way. This modern idea is also championed by modern, feminized males. These men want to usurp authority over single women, misusing them for their pleasure, without the "price" of marital provisions and protections. Some of these men and women ignorantly equate a woman with sexual standards (not bowing to whimsical urges) as being escort-like. These individuals are obviously not well-read, nor do they understand the depth of intimacy. A woman's body is to be highly regarded, by her first, and then by others. Even looking at history, dowries were prevalent in certain parts of the world. It goes without saying that a woman's values are indeed "priceless"; however, a woman should not be devalued by removing a method of exchange.

The "wholesome" order is that the male offers his services as a husband and an agreeing female offers her services as a wife. Both must serve, and serving one another is costly. The price is time, money, and other valuable resources. A few centuries ago, not even women of the night (prostitutes) willingly participated in free sensual encounters. This would have shown a belittling of her as a human, on par with sexual violation. Most immoral women would only participate in sensual activity "in exchange" for things such as a higher position in society, better housing arrangements, and a steady income supplied from the prominent males. The reason is obvious. What is considered valuable enough to seek out, will always cost a price. Therefore, as there was and is a price for immoral women, there is undoubtedly a cost for moral, traditional women. The cost is legal marriage.

While it is known that casual sex causes casualties, due to western culture, there are modern men who voice disdain if not allowed this accommodation after dates. It should go without saying that women, on initial "get to know you" outings, should have no expectancy of expensive, unbudgeted dates. If the date is for clean purposes, with mutual clear motives, she should not want or expect a man to be an "early husband", spending bill-level money. She is not in the classification of a fiancé or wife. The expense of these extravagant dating styles (with uncommitted people) is part of the reason certain men "expect" intimacy as earned and implied. This mindset mainly snuck in from the free love movement, solidifying among the agreeing dating participants. Traveling along the "backwards culture way", both male and female values eroded to believe strange things. Men and women who choose to date this way, can and will continue these thought patterns and behaviors that produce the rotten fruit or barrenness of those seeds.

Many in conservative spaces charge latter-wave feminists as the sole culprit for why modern men do not value intimacy or marriage. What is troubling is that there are not enough mothers and fathers bold enough to inform their daughters of the wiles of an "immature" male, along with the purpose of sexual integrity. Feminist women ushered in the desensitization of intimacy by stripping away its sacredness. They opened the door for modern men to run right in and over to agreeing women who believe themselves free and empowered from lack of inhibition. In a witnessed interview of a popular rapper, the rapper admitted that money and fame gave him access to excessive amounts of women. He went on to state that by having slept with so many willing women, he no longer values the act of sex and can do without it. While this seems great if he will now take the abstinence journey, what is disturbing is that there are other men and women who feel this way. These are people who have reduced the value of a God-approved and instituted act by engaging in it out of order, haphazardly. When men and women view sex as "ordinary", or just a physical thing, they lower the value of it, along with the standards of access to it. This in turn, depreciates the act between those participants.

One might ask, "What would make our alleged female empowerment leaders promote such a heinous agenda that harms an important part of a woman's "honor"?" The same feminist leaders also claim concern for women's mental, physical, and reproductive health, while ignoring the high sexually transmitted infection rates of women in casual sex and open, multiple partner relationships, void of sexual boundaries. Feminists callously turn a blind eye and look to distort data on the overwhelming amount of women who report feelings of misuse, guilt, and brokenness behind years of having casual intimate partners. Under the feminist movement's mantra of free, uninhibited sex, there appears to be found no individual or community benefits. Many concerned critics name the overwhelming negative results yielded. Sources reveal women experience "mixed signals" more than men, in relation to premarital sex encounters. These mixed signals lead to insecurity, loneliness, depression, and anxiety in women. For those who believe in spirituality, the other presented danger is the "soul tie" (sharing of a strong emotional, physical, and spiritual "attachment") with sensual partners. Soul ties strengthen the argument that sex always comes with some form of cost. Women are noted to explore their emotions more intensely than men. This is due to a female's biological makeup, which influences human behaviors. This knowledge supports the red flag of "hook-up culture" harming, not charming, women. The female, by created design, is "internal" and the recipient of male penetration. Always remember that many things of value are "hidden" from the casual eye on and for "purpose". Forming attachment bonds with limitless partners does not promote mental, physical, or spiritual wellness.

Young women of present day need to know that a barrier to entry is still necessary. Standards always set people apart from others. A woman does not have to subject herself to becoming any man's side or secret relationship. Also, it should never be a stigma or uncommon to remain abstinent in whatever age range while waiting for marriage and "meaningful" sensual relations. Popularizing the old fallacy of sleeping around with no consequence serves an immature male's fantasy. This should never have had any part in feminism. The fact that it does, is conspicuous. What is valued must be protected and not dealt with carelessly.

Even though men are not the main audience addressed in this book, many ladies may ask, "Shouldn't males hold intimacy standards?" They absolutely should. Men also must be taught from their youth to establish boundaries for themselves, exercising sexual discipline and restraint. Who a man gives his DNA to, risking procreation, must be a wise choice. When he holds values for himself, he will ensure the woman is also found worthy of him and his seeds. He must also perform character and behavior examinations. A woman's worthiness should never be naively based on her physical appearance alone. A man's health, finances, and this female dominated culture, warrant him to exercise caution and discipline. He is the first controller of his future offspring as he chooses the mother of his children.

Further reflecting on the downward spiral of modern culture, a few years ago there was a raved television show (aired 2012-2018) displaying a female minority lead by the character name of Olivia Pope. From a resume standpoint, this woman was well educated, successful, attractive, affable, and clever. With all of these positive attributes, she sadly exhibited a desire for relational chaos and drama. This character passed over several viable suitors and engagements to single men that would have given her what she "stated" that she wanted: stability, marriage, children, and a home with a white picket fence. It is important to point out here that inventory must be taken of our daily actions (behaviors) to see if they line up with our professed statements (speech). Presumably, Ms. Pope was in her late 30s to early 40s. Instead of boarding the plane for the life she had "full access to" then, and years prior, Ms. Pope chose to continually submit to and entangle herself with a complex, unhappily married man of high power and position. This placed Ms. Pope in a compromised position of weakness, as a trophy on his shelf. The alarm was that she allowed herself to be placed there.

It was also reported that in one season of the show, they advertised Ms. Pope terminating her unborn child. This must have been a timely and purposeful maneuver to blend with the favored modern narrative of children being destructive to career success. How depraved it is that the writers knew what messages to persuade and sell to their targeted audience of women at that particular time. Was another message that women should play second place (the other/side woman) or take another number instead to a man? Even if the intent was to portray an intelligent, flawed, and relatable character, how does this representation positively showcase the "image" of minority women, specifically unmarried career women? Surely the viewers did not expect a cookie-cutter character, but the decided continual character flaws (relational indecisiveness, adultery, and premarital sex) did not need broadcasting for the audience to believe that they occur.

What other reason than profit motive would this storyline be promoted to women and women of color? Presenting drama and dysfunction is often lucrative. In reality, the average successful career woman behaving this way in relationships sorely regrets her choices later in life. Ms. Pope is representative of select women who prefer the aroma of someone else's ready-made pie over actually preparing and consuming their own. This alleged empowerment figure wasted years of time and energy, giving emotions to a "dream". The character's role did not appear to be written to focus on the state of her present and future actuality. Furthermore, Ms. Pope was referred to as a crisis handler. Ironically, she was titled "head of the gladiators (her problem-solving associates)". In Roman history, a gladiator was highly trained, armed, and skilled for combat and violent confrontations with criminals, wild animals, and even other gladiators. Ms. Pope did not exert her gladiator training or skills to solve her own life's conundrum in the way that she did for others. She neglected adherence to boundaries that would have mitigated loss of valuable time. In this character's life, the true gladiator mentality would have slayed the wild ideas of temporal fantasies being more alluring than the stability and soundness of an honorable, fulfilling life formed with her own husband and children. .

In driving the point home, it is always best for women who desire marriage and children to arrive timely to board their "first" flight (marriage opportunity). The "check- in" process secures the seat. If not secured, another woman can take that seat. If ladies miss or pass on check-in to stay in the dating pool longer (entertaining "distraction" relationships), they are detoured into stagnancy (youth years and potentially high-quality suitors lost). This delay mandates that these women plan to reschedule the flight, which can come with a fee. Although the next flight options may not be as preferable, the desired destination has not changed. Aim not to miss the original flight. Many media outlets deceive women, promoting several extremes. One extreme is that women should forever physically look 21 years old, thus, they should try out all the latest beauty regimes (skin rejuvenation, Botox, and other more dangerous plastic surgeries) in efforts to meet this "secular standard". Another extreme is that "life ends after 40". Both are inaccurate, as they fail to highlight what qualities should be developed in each age range and what traits should be extolled as important. Physical beauty is not the only thing a man is looking for from a 40 plus year old woman, but it definitely may be sufficient and what he is captured by from a 25 year old. Modern media platforms speak deception in making women believe they can "demand" the same things at age 50 that they could at age 25. Those are different ages and phases of a woman's life. Each age range has its' own flavor, uniqueness, and learned experiences. The same media influencers, females and males, are guilty of promoting physical beauty as the end all be all. Of course, everyone should take care of their skin and body, but overall health is more important than physical appearance alone. We must ensure the development of excellent character and wisdom in each age group. As women age, these count more when weighed in the balance.

Looking further into the various dating and marriage trends, people continue to believe that dating is evolving. In times past, it was known that a man was required to meet a young woman's father or other male family leader for approval (vetting). By previous generations and traditional groups of women today, courting is esteemed a more respectable form of dating in a well-functioning society. This is due to restrictions of what the female and male were allowed to do, and the end result of "no dignity lost" from either party if a marriage did not ensue. Courting held men to standards. It required men to establish themselves financially beforehand and then to "win or woo" the desired woman for honorable purposes. Courting specifically focused on getting to know the other person to decide if they were a possible marital mate. Sexual activity during this time would have clouded judgment and caused private and public shame if the two did not marry. This standard was noted to show decreased rates of children born outside of marriage as the unwedded birth rates were significantly lower than present day. Courtship was known to be either informal, between the male and female, or formal, arranged with family approval for betrothal. It was common to see adult chaperones accompanying any family agreed upon courting for public dates. The Silent Generation women were likely to have continued courting, depending on morals and social class; however, there was emergence of high school and college students starting to date multiple people, of which was called "playing the field", leading up to World War II. This was a competitive dating style where they chose to date who was popular and connected among their peers.

As years passed, Baby Boomers participated in the American style of dating known as "Going steady", during and after World War II. This style was more romance driven and prevalent from the 1950s through part of the 1980s. Going steady was also trendy in high schools and colleges, replacing the competitive and popularity-oriented dating style that swarmed after courting. Studies of these young adults showed that going steady was approved of as the style of dating by those whose goal was marriage and by those who had no aim of marriage, simply viewing this dating style as appropriate social relationship behavior. Going steady was cited to give a form of status akin to engagement by it being secluded to one male and one female. It was considered off limits for another male to attempt to date a female involved in a going steady relationship. This implied respect was given from even outsiders and peers regarding the seriousness of the couple's relationship because intent was specified in the going steady relationships positioned for marriage.

Women are negatively affected by the current condition of American dating that decreases the possibility of a healthy relationship. As earlier referenced, one of the main reasons is the lack of proper checking forces. Pamela Thomas, author of *Fatherless Daughters*, posited that women who grew up with absent fathers find it difficult to form lasting relationships. The rejection of fathers can scar and produce a fear of rejection from other men. Our society sees examples of this with the consumed career-oriented woman, stating contempt of establishing a family, and with the overtly sexual woman, who holds no "protective" standards. Self-protective measures are instituted, and inner walls are built to prevent the possibility of further damage from men. The onset of masculine-like behaviors occur in some scorned women. As reiterated, the guidance and leadership of a father or father figure is essential for filtering possible marital mates. Fathers must also teach daughters about respect and boundaries for themselves and men. Numerous studies reveal that young ladies with absent or unstable fathers are more likely to participate in nonmarital intimacy, as well as engage in risky sexual behaviors. This creates economic and social issues for women, leading to unplanned pregnancies outside of marriage, limitless pregnancy terminations for some, higher likelihood of poverty, and recurrent unsubstantial relationships. God designed women to be "covered" under the umbrella of love, protection, and provision that He first provides, and then charges a man to provide in marriage. Today, the social culture appeals to the emotions (which are temporal and ever-changing) of women instead of meeting the embedded natural needs for them. In order to do the latter, it would require "application" of care and concern for women, not just lip service.

A November of 2022 Brigham Young University (BYU) article on the dangers of dating applications(apps), discussed how a study led by a BYU nurse linked dating apps to 14 percent of female sexual assault victims from the years 2017 to 2020. College aged women were more likely to be victimized on first dates who used dating apps for meetups with the targeted females possessing mental illnesses and other vulnerabilities. It is known that dating apps have served some individuals positively in helping to meet compatible partners for a relationship leading to marriage. We must also recognize that there are other dating applications, "App Traps" if you will, developed and geared to harm and objectify women. They reduce the date meetups to casual sex with numerous people, alleging no strings attached. Sources revealed that Tinder, Bumble, Grindr, BLK, and the like, were cited to encourage one-night stand, risky behaviors and prey on the emotions of vulnerable women. Many dating apps propagate women being temporary thrills, sinisterly aiming to artificially appease women's natural desire to be needed and confirmed. Western women have been indoctrinated, predominantly by the cruel intentioned, to believe a "do what thou whilst" mentality is empowering, attempting to compare it against being in a stable, committed relationship with a spouse.

As afore highlighted, certain music artists endorsed and created degrading messages towards females, desensitizing males to women's virtues. From the 1980s until early 2000s, Madonna (a Baby Boomer), was proclaimed to be a key icon and sexual freedom symbol for other Baby Boomers, Generation X, and Millennial women. She was a world-known singer stated to publicly push the limits on promiscuity and gender fluidity by creating and scantily performing vulgar songs, releasing an erotica book titled *Sex*, and tongue kissing a younger mentee, singer, Britney Spears, on stage, to name a few. She contributed to making it more acceptable for future female music artists (known to mimic her edgy fashion styles and mannerisms) to continue increasing their presentation of these ideals of womanhood to their audience of "everyday" women. Some of the female music artists who create cringe lyrics and lewd videos are secretly married, engaged, or pursuing a stable, monogamous relationship. They feed aspiring young girls and women a diet of falsities, promoting independence (instead of interdependence), being single, emotionally unregulated, overuse of Plan B pills, damaging pregnancy terminations, and engaging with multiple sex partners. The motive for this was and still is profit. The "Independence" message sells well and strikes gold among Generation X, Millennial, and Generation Z single females because it provides a sense of "false comfort and validation". It must be reiterated that most female artists do not live the "image they sell" to other women. Discernment has been numbed. Unfortunately, some women are simply unable to detect when they are being misled, coddled, and lulled to sleep while purging inhibition, standards, and values for the new "it things" socially accepted. The methodical presentation of messages from celebrities and other influencers carries social weight. Continual messaging to young women of wild fun and life being monotonous partying and flings, i.e., "throwing yourself to the wolves", releases a negative and overgeneralized view of a woman's hallmark.

Women should never feel pressured to be anyone's negative entertainment. As long as there is breath in the body, it is never too late to chart out and start a new path. Countless testimonials are circulating on social media of women who participated in the independent, sexual deviant revolution and turned away from it. Increasingly women are speaking out against immoral cultures, declaring their regret of unveiling themselves on Instagram, Only Fans, chatrooms, and before numerous people for sensual encounters. Some of these ladies now desire a traditional lifestyle, a husband, and to be cared for after those years of running from, what other feminist women proclaim, is "outdated thinking".

By definition, a "gender war" is predominantly between biological males and females. The female asserts the narrative that most or all men are cheaters, abusers, misogynistic, and uncaring. The men believe most or all women to be artificial, self-serving, unthankful, cheaters, and abandoners of soft skills and wifely qualities. Numerous online media content creators continue making financial gains from spreading divisive messaging. They prefer to "feed the lion" of gender war conflict. It is never good to consume or create content that "glorifies dysfunction" among created order sexes, for the sake of the mighty dollar. Are there platforms with panels where men and women civilly discuss relationship topics? Absolutely, however, the discussions with vitriol, stereotypical behavior, rudeness, and tearing down of the other person should not be consumed. They are "entertainment only", aimlessly arguing with no end goal towards rectifying behaviors that "cause" the relational issues at topic. Media has the power to imprint on the soul. What you consume, you believe, and become. The demeaning and irate male and female conversations tend to circulate virally, while the polite and respectful female and male dialogues "offering solutions" are less recommended by the algorithm.

4

Return of the Basics: Ode to Foundations

Adults who come into maturity, broaden their thinking. They develop optimism for the ability of males and females appropriately functioning as individuals, and in healthy relationships. The surprise for some is, this calls for "personal changes" and a reestablishment of the abandoned roles and functions for each to produce the constructive, collective results. Yes, those roles, attributes, and abilities that latter-day feminists believe to limit or weaken women, are actually many of her true strengths. It is necessary to seek therapy and wise counsel while addressing persistent issues that have caused, or are a potential for detriment, to women's future relationships. There is no need to continually argue with one another on social platforms expressing the relationship issues. It's time to fix them. Anyone who is not in the solutions business is in the business of keeping the drama and trauma going, which happens to be more profitable. God created males and females to fulfill His purpose and carry out vision. For the spiritually minded, it is known that the plan of the Adversary is to cause strife, disdain, bitterness, and lasting wedges between the sexes to thwart the woman's seed (children) from bruising the Enemy's head (book of Genesis 3:15).

Single and divorced women have complained for years that there are no respectable men worth seriously dating, let alone marrying. Many are stating that gentlemen no longer exist. One must also fairly question if gentlewomen still exist. If they do, are they positioned in life and present in the settings to meet respectable caliber men? As of 2023, the definition of a "gentleman" is referred to as a chivalrous, honorable, and courteous man. He is a man possessing good and courteous conduct. A June 9, 2023 New York Post article discussed a self-proclaimed "liberal" woman who rapidly circulated on TikTok stating that she could not seem to find a traditional, masculine man who was also liberal. She proclaimed that the men with masculine qualities (wanting to pay on first dates, open her car door, and who desire to care and provide for her) were mainly "conservative" men in beliefs. She went on to say that she wanted a partner who does not expect her to conform to traditional female roles (cooking, cleaning, being a homemaker, or childbearing). The California woman did state that she expected traditional things from the man (which would seem to imply mutual exchanges). Perhaps, she and other like-minded women who believe horror stories pertaining strictly to traditional or conservative men, would consider stepping outside of their comfort zones, researching, and laying to rest these false beliefs and claims that latter feminists propagate.

Gentlemen do exist today. There are men, predominantly in traditional, religious settings, who adhere to following principles and ethics that work to push the functioning of the man's life and the lives of a wife, children, and community. A gentleman is selfless. In traditional households, it is common for many men to open car doors, maintenance cars and homes, take out the trash, help change baby diapers, and help with children's homework. These valuable men may work blue collar trades, be in corporate America, own businesses, as well as perform in other ways our current culture considers traditional and limiting.

For the past 30 plus years, it has been regarded wrong and biased to establish gender norms, or to assign a male or female a set of functions to fulfill. Of course, a woman can mow grass and a man can cook meals. These types of things do not take away from femininity or masculinity as there are things that one partner can do in better quality than the other. The end goal is functionality and purpose being accomplished. Structures and systems help guide a relationship and home environment. A physical home that is built on a "solid foundation" is sure to stand. The first step to building a physical house is to clear the way and lay the foundation. The strength and stability of the structure, hinges on its' foundation. Looking at this from a relationship standpoint, how can a man and woman's home be established and stand against the issues of life, with no guidelines or playbook? This proves the notion of everyone going their own way, doing what "feels" right, removing fundamentals, principles, and standards, is preposterous. All other important aspirations humans have, they research, learn, and "follow a plan" on how to acquire and maintain them. What makes substantial relationships any different?

Foundations are powerful. A society that veers so far away from any form of fundamentals and structures, induces confusion and chaos in dating relationships. The idea of marrying someone becomes loathsome. With the eradication of gender or sex associated roles for the female, this inadvertently removed the traditional expectations for the male. What people fail to understand is, if a woman can abandon an entire set of established, distinguishable functions (that promote a family's success), so can and has the modern man. This may have been an intentional plan from hidden powerful figures. There are non-traditional or liberal men (latter Boomers, Generation X, Millennials, and Gen Z) who were raised by single, divorced, or dysfunctional married parents. The female parents of these men were likely under strong feminist influence. The way in which men are reared, influences their behaviors and beliefs through phases of life in the same way it impacts females.

Hopefully, it will not take many more years before it becomes clear that in order for single women who desire marriage to have what they desire, they must become the complementary version of it. This demands a return to foundations that build and sustain. Everything in life is a give and take. Who would have thought that women cooking, cleaning, homeschooling, working remote, or deciding to be a homemaker (housewife), were crime-like insults to your womanhood? Should not every adult know how to prepare food and be cleanly, without hostility or pity being directed at them? According to modern, feminist culture, a woman who is good at, or enjoys homely things, is not in tune with her true self or is dreadfully unhappy. It is apparent that these feminists do not engage with working women to know that they also experience feelings of doubt, entrapment, unfulfillment, and unhappiness, giving their years of time and energy (service) to workplace ladder climbing. On either side of the aisle, housewife or corporate/businesswoman, there is no escaping these occasional doubts and frustrations that all women have at points in their lives.

In the "seasons of life", all people experience changes of feelings, thoughts, or beliefs. With aging, physical health and hormone variations are contributors of various female emotions and behaviors, when unmanaged. Prayer, proper healthcare, mentorship, networking, and therapy are imperative. Feelings are often variable. Solely trusting and acting on irresolute feelings is unwise and destructive. Consider that only children act on feelings, impulsively dropping responsibilities (chores or studying) to pursue treats or playtime (temporary satisfaction).

Joy is synonymous with happiness; however, joy is a jubilance not predicated on outside circumstances. Learning to possess joy will always be more fulfilling than happiness. Happiness is temporal. It is solely emotions and feelings oriented because it is based on happenings. To pursue a constant state of happiness will require persistent searching for the occurrences that produce these fleeting feelings. Joy is an internal surety that comes with comfort and peace, highly needed in life's times of chaos and uncertainty. Women who possess joy are not dependent on, or swayed, by external sources. They have an internal optimism.

Traditional-leaning women are unfortunately viewed by modern culture as limited and antiquated. What is a known fact is that antiques happen to be rare in supply, yet sought after all over the world. Who would not want to be considered an antique and "set apart" when females outnumber males in most American states? The definition of an "antique" is an item perceived as having high value. It is referred to as a treasure, collector's item, and period piece. Any wise mother or positive female figure for young ladies would promote the value of a woman conducting herself as an antique, rather than modish. Trends and styles come and go, but the lasting value of antiques places them in another class than what is common and fashionable at the time. An antique woman will be at the front of the line for suitors because she is a rarity.

It is long overdue for debunking of false claims that a traditional minded person believes women are to be barefoot, pregnant, and in the kitchen. For years, fear tactic messages have permeated as factual in western spheres. Everyone is aware of innocent women who bravely told and tell of their horrible, abusive experiences while involved with cult-like group practices (that should always be condemned, and the leaders held accountable). Society continues to market the atrocious experiences of these women as a fear campaign to all women relaying: "See there woman. That will happen to you.". Such maneuvers are evil and disingenuous. These negative experiences do not regularly transpire in a non-hypocritical, healthy, loving, and Christ-following union, encompassing preestablished boundaries and shared principles.

Middle and senior aged women should activate their calling. It is vital that they come out of competition with younger women, and into wisdom and compassion, teaching young ladies how to cultivate and exemplify their "enduring" values. The "Desperate Housewives" depiction of middle aged women promotes the behaviors and beliefs that this age group of women are to be messy, hyperemotional, vain, self-serving, and destructive. Those women are rich and their predominant audience is not, yet they still promote the drama that the average woman's life will suffer from if she mimics them. That is not the "Helpmate" image our Creator had in mind, as these behaviors do not aid in showing forth a woman's values. These presentations may "get the views", but they distort the mind of the consumers. Our real world needs real, mature women who will stand against consuming negative broadcasted portrayals of them. As previously mentioned, how women are portrayed, often influences how they are viewed and treated by the same and opposite sex. It's time to change the narrative.

Seasoned women must also teach ladies that allowing men to have free, uncommitted access to hallowed "restricted zones", chips away at their vessels. Taking on humility and adapting what elder women call, a "teachable spirit", is necessary for younger women to receive instructions on how to develop and thrive in their natural femininity. When returning to foundations that build, it is pertinent that girls and women in training be instructed on how to establish standards for how they adorn and carry themselves, serve others, and convey respect in communication. For young women who did not grow up in a household where these important elements were discussed or exemplified, it plays out in their adulthood relationships. Community mentorship, leadership, etiquette training programs, as well as faith-based groups, prove helpful in training young girls, contributing to a decreased influence of detached celebrity influencers. In order to truly empower women and the next generation, they have to be prepared for "the real world, real life, and real relationships", not the life of the rich and star-studded few, who may be compensated heftily to endorse what destroys the general woman.

Could there already be a revival of modern women returning to what some fundamental religious or spiritual group women still practice? As referenced, an emergence of women on social platforms such as TikTok, Instagram, and YouTube are denouncing the lies of being fulfilled solely from their career achievements. They appear to be having an "epiphany moment", revealing that they now have desires to be loved and share their lives with a traditional, monogamous spouse. Some of these women profess to be entering their "Soft Girl or Soft Living Era". This encompasses deviating from the pressure of being obsessively in control and career focused, to participate in self-care, proper diet and exercise, enjoying or cultivating healthy relationships, and learning to create a peaceful, soft version of themselves. The era is understood to market traditional, feminine mannerisms and making choices that exude daintiness. Soft Girl living women began and are embracing the mental and life shift that chooses gentleness over combativeness and conflict. They are rightfully rejecting the permeating idea that in order for a woman to fulfill purpose and have success, she must adapt "hardness" and masculine idiosyncrasies (which unintentionally repel attracting a masculine man for a serious relationship or marriage).

Some feminist supporting critics claim the Soft Girl movement to be a rebellious detriment to the success of latter feminist movements. Feminists admonish women to always be in control of a situation, wearing numerous hats at the same time. This feminist mentality unwittingly runs feminist women into a continual stupor. Female supporters of the Soft Girl movement confirm that it is always a great thing for women to come out of fight or flight mode, receive wellness, and smell the roses, so to speak. Proponents view the movement as crucial, kindling women's choice to be feminine, embracing who she was created to be.

Another popular countermovement to radical feminism is known by a social media TikTok hashtag "TradWife" (traditional wife). According to a January of 2023 report from the New York Post, these women overly reject modern feminism. They seek to adopt a more 1950s style of housewife. Whether these women are actually taking on these beliefs in their private lives, or simply for social media attention to garner profit, the TradWife hashtag has already amassed over 110 million views. These women assert that they are not pushing their view of following traditional female roles on other women; however, they are hoping to provide insight and a chance to view the lifestyle through another lens. A March of 2023 Essence article discussed how the trend to become a traditional stay-at-home mother and wife could be problematic. Opposing women voice that managing the household and relinquishing the financial obligation reigns, leaves women vulnerable, and that while submitting to the care of the household and others, these women will neglect and let themselves go.

Traditional social media content creators have gained large viewership and popularity over the years. It appears that women are hungry and searching for something wholesome and of substance. They do not see themselves as the counterculture, but rather the remnant representation of what was normally done by women across the world for thousands of years. Instead of "adding to", latter wave feminists, "set a fire" to distinguishable aspects of womanhood. Traditional-leaning women on YouTube and TikTok are using their influence to instruct on topics such as homesteading, home schooling, family budgeting, organizing, decorating, modest apparel, cooking, cleaning, being a loving wife, and attentive child rearing. It is refreshing to observe certain social media personalities successfully dominating in this niche, as a desire to revive some of what was judged old-fashioned, may be here to stay for the foreseeable future. Social platforms and conferences make it much easier to connect with like-minded individuals and groups, as well as provide an opportunity for latter wave feminists to learn and experience what they furiously believe to be an oppressive, alternative way of existence.

5

Social Advantage of the Shift

Pivoting is not always easy. It often comes with malaise. Naming the many strengths of women comes naturally. It is a fact that women were active and influential long before they finally received public recognition for all that they contribute. Virtuous women have always been a bedrock in their family and communities. When nations were and are involved in war, forcing men to the battle zones, helpful women chose and still choose to stand in the gap, unfortunately striving to fill "provision and nurturing shoes". Women with disabled or long-term illness suffering spouses, step up to the plate daily ensuring their homes needs are met. These examples and more, attest to the distinctive significance of women and their need meeting capacity. Any attempt, specifically from other women, to "blur the lines" and discredit a woman's values, functions, and contributions, is hateful and against divine order. Removing positive elements of womanhood that demonstrate women's notability and distinction from men, is a treacherous slope. It eventually removes protections for women, taking them back to where they believed to have progressed from. These things eerily welcome women's replacement with self-proclaiming replicas, as removing or dismissing renowned, innate characteristics, can cause a social culture where natural women feel obsolete.

Perceiving modern norms, women, at the hands of third and fourth wave feminists, are being pushed out. These latter feminists promote other causes in place of their originated unique purpose of solely focusing on expansion of rights and equality for females. According to some critics, latter wave feminists' current supported causes aim to wittedly replace a woman's necessary and established place in society. If females are not the only ones who can (generally) menstruate, breastfeed, or be impregnated, then the door does appear to be wide open for the possibility of what critics speculate. Further, if the argument and angry point of contention was and is that "This is a man's (male dominated) world.", surely feminist women would not want or allow men to infiltrate the movement that their first wave feminist predecessors fought to institute (due to various oppressions from males).

The benefits are insurmountable when women journey into or continue their walk of embracing their created fullness. Referring back to history, women held influence over their children. This is contrary to the current peddled message for women to move away from care of the home's affairs and into the race of corporate ladder ascension. Can a woman manage her home's needs, excel in the workplace, establish a thriving business, and have time to pour back into her own well-being? Yes, but can it be done without burnout, or the needs of her family being neglected? A December of 2020 CNBC article addressed that being a working mother made women 28 percent more likely to experience burnout, which was specified to be higher among Black, Asian, and Latin American women. The article continued that burnout among working women was a problem among minority women well before the COVID pandemic. Women are deserving of rest and self-care. This appears to be an equal issue whether women solely work inside their homes or additionally outside of their homes.

Women are often hailed as great behind the scenes and forefront multitaskers. This is a fact; however, it must be stressed that women functioning in excessive exhaustion (depleted) mode should only be done in seasons such as war time, family emergencies, health crisis, and the like. No feminist woman or man should place the loaded burden of daily "fight or flight, hat juggling" solely on women as a method of proving their strength and abilities. While thinking of women "coming to the rescue" for their families, the reason numerous women's purses are so large is because they have first aid kits, stain cleaners, needle and thread for clothes repairs, snacks for small children, mints, bottled water, wet wipes for spills, face rags, and Kleenex. If these items are not in their purse, they are more than likely in their car. This may be a simple referenced example for laughs, but it yields proof that properly trained women are always thinking about the needs of others. Instructed women are known to prepare for a multitude of unexpected things. They have the ability to make an uncomfortable situation better than it would have been without their presence. Useful women appear to be superheroes and often save the day. The superwoman movie may fail to display that the woman also needs to rest and recharge. Men and women who "produce" worthy works, must be poured back into.

Let's discuss real power moves. As aforementioned, putting the idea of casual sex to bed, is long overdue. A common saying is that, "Women control access to sex (upon her agreement or consent) and men control access to marriage (through his proposal to her)". Women have always had power in the dating phase and they could increase marriage percentages if they individually and collectively agreed to do so. The writing on the wall is, why would males rush to legally marry women if they are being given marriage benefits immediately before and during the dating phase? Realizing that females have a high level of control in this area also makes females responsible for their part in the individual and collective outcomes of the current dating trends producing less marriages. Understand that women with no requirements for sexual access ruin the chances of engagement for other women desiring marriage. This grim mirror-facing reality is the result of the extensive availability and promotion of premarital sex in western culture. If all women exercised their power of restraint, it would positively affect the dating culture for mature, purposeful daters. Women must establish or revive a relational code of ethics and integrity.

Another vital power move towards women's actual progression is refusing the lifestyle or trap of cohabitation (living together unmarried). This is synonymous with being in a "situationship" or gray area. It has the presence of fun, but the absence of marital benefits, commitment, norms, and defined expectations. A Pew Research Center study revealed a 2019 survey presenting that 69 percent of Americans believe cohabitation to be acceptable without the plan of marriage. The article conveyed that among those aged 18 to 44, about 59 percent have lived with an unmarried partner while only 50 percent have ever been married, per the National Survey of Family Growth. A situationship can either feel light-hearted, with no "visible" strings attached, or it can be a costly emotional rollercoaster.

Contrary to popular belief, legal marriage in the United States is still a protection for most women, and it is owed when upstanding women and men desire to become sexually involved, risking procreation with one another. Strong prenuptial agreements can be put in place to remove the extensive loss of income and standard of living as excuses from either party as reasons not to legally marry. Centuries ago, there were no genetic tests to determine paternity. A woman and her children received honor, inheritance, land, and position through the institution of legal marriage. For a man (or feminist in disguise) to short a deserving woman of the legal title and support of a wife, calling marriage a progressive and man-made government institution, is erroneous and foolish. This mindset takes women backwards, inadvertently implying that their bodies are wanted, however, they serve no greater functions in a man's life. The "it's just an institution" argument should be unacceptable at this point. No moral man would want his daughter subjected to living and caring for a man she is not legally married to. He inwardly knows that marriage comes with a "covering and benefits". Some of these cohabitating men pass away, selfishly leaving the woman and their children without due resources from his bank accounts, life insurance policies, wills, or trusts. Connection to a woman's mind, time, resources, and body, without the reciprocity of a legal joining, deprives the woman of what she is worth.

Another observance is that there seems to be a female and male fear of the term "commitment", often due to damage from past failed relationships. There are those who are inclined to believe that commitment to a marriage is supposed to inhibit, suffocate, and oppress them. A healthy marriage does not do this, but a trauma filled relationship, married or unmarried, will. Due to this awareness, it is for the best that females and males have single seasons during their healing phase to prevent relational dead weight or trauma carrying. It is also necessary to prevent trauma bonding (connecting through one another's painful energy), a yoke that is difficult for many to sever. Requesting a woman to pause her life and wait for a man to possibly "come around" to the action of marriage, is unfair and improper. No one's lifespan "pauses" for them to get something together. A female's egg does not pause leaving her body each month to give a man time to get his life's affairs in order, or to choose a proper relationship with her. Time is a precious commodity, more valuable than money. Commitment simply implies dedication and taking responsibility for something, or someone, found and proclaimed as worthy of choosing.

It is appalling that there are also men who prepare themselves (using these years- long situationships) to propel, or ignorantly demote, to new women altogether. This is witnessed regularly in current culture and it is socially accepted. These men are not socially shamed for this "bounce

41

around" behavior. It is without a doubt, when a man is ready, he will do what is right by a chosen woman. A female lowering her anchor for years to empty promises, cohabitating with a "not ready or never ready" male, experiences heartbreak and bitterness. The "serious" males who are actively pursuing marital mates, overlook cohabitating women, believing the relationships they are in with the uncommitted men to be serious ones. Men with deceptive motives are cognizant that living together gives loyal-natured women the "presentation" of a serious relationship status. In a sense, undecided men place a cohabitating woman "on standby". In his mind, she's off the dating or marriage market. The deception is that sharing keys is supposedly indicative of a valued status among cohabitors.

Although feminist, senior aged women do not readily have heart to heart talks with younger women on how to prepare the mind and body for "the shift/change of life", it is important to reiterate that women do possess a biological fertility clock. This should not be looked upon as a loss or something shameful for women. It is simply a "notification" to one of life's many transitions. Men and women experience "shifts" with the blessing of aging. For those women desiring of marriage, casual relationships or play time throughout the mid-twenties, thirties, and forties is misguided. It is not equitable for society to expect females to spare 2, 3, 5, 10 or more years with one man, or rotations of men, waiting to be chosen. These women accumulate experiences that imprint memories. These memories, good, bad, or ugly, will follow these men and women. Females should be aware that males are not restricted by the same reproductive clock that women are. Yes, males' health is also an inhibitor as they age as it pertains to them procreating in those age ranges. Children born to senior aged men have higher risks of developmental issues the same as with an older mother. An older man's sole advantage is financial. Males typically earn higher incomes or have more income streams as they continue to head further into their forties, fifties, and sixties. This already attained financial security makes these middle and senior aged men more appealing (and often a target) to females who are 10 to 25 years younger than them.

No woman has to allow herself to be hidden or reserved for the possibility of commitment that may never occur. Most religious or spiritual followers believe that a relationship is only serious with proposal and engagement in place. Other traditional people may go as far as to say a woman is not completely out of the dating market until she is actually legally married. With either belief, wisdom speaks and says to leave the undisciplined, untrusting, uncommitted modern man in the dating pool for other modern women (whose choice may also be to never marry).

The condition of many households should prove the need for active, present women in their homes. Women are imperative to the development of children, particularly as a forcefield against secular, negative social influencers. When children are reared in a marital household where the couple shares similar beliefs, values, and core methods for developing a loving and stable home environment, children are more likely to have the confidence and belief that they can succeed outside of the home. A January of 2021 report from Deseret News discussed the reasons why children deserve the privilege of a strong two- parent household. It posited the child having increased chances of financial security, higher grades and extracurricular involvement, decreased chances of alcohol, drug, or sexual abuse, a decreased chance of engagement in risky sexual activity, and a reduction of committing crimes in the juvenile justice system. Research shows that a stable two-parent home structure has not been the norm for decades. This is due to the prevalence of rotational relationships children witness their parents involved in, and are inadvertently raised in.

A woman's positive impact in her home and community is not an "unnecessary past time". Latter wave feminists foolishly reduce the value of conventional roles and functions as restrictive and lacking importance. What they fail to realize is that a woman who puts God, her health, family, and others as a priority, will be praised and honored before she leaves this Earth. Who happily remembers or respects women who choose not to exemplify honorable and noteworthy behaviors that are a benefit and service to others? Not many people. A reverenced woman will be the female educator who brings personal hygiene or food items to discreetly give to students in need. The mother who serves her household well, and her children become prominent in society, will be praised for her labor. The aunt, grandmother, or sibling who steps in to care for relatives' children, they will be honored. The female foster or adoptive parents who demonstrate the love of God by taking in orphan children to give them better lives, will be highly cherished because of their great sacrifice and caring heart. A wisdom seeking woman will examine the personal lives of latter wave feminists in comparison to traditional, role carrying women. Whose lives present more fruit (beneficial results)?

There is no fulfillment gained throwing away harmless feminine traits in pursuit of self-centered ambitions and the desires of the workplace. Some corporations can and will continue replacing women (and anyone) they have collected years of virtue and value from. Also, female self-started businesses with the best efforts and attention, can unfortunately still fail. Never discredit the return on investment of starting and maintaining a marriage, home, and family. Children become adults and those adults can either become constructive or destructive to the creation of a safe and productive society. The content of daily news reports prove this. Modern women should discern how identity and temperament issues among children and current adults are heavily correlated with broken homes, void of adequate love, structures, and designated functions. The decades of "do what you want", and "everyone goes and makes their own way" cultural approaches, have simply not produced positive results for the women who utilize them as mothers, nor for the daughters reared under these philosophies.

Without the attention, nurture, and guidance of women in the home, the child and eventual adult are likely to gravitate towards anything (vices) and anyone (improper relationships) for a sense of belonging and purpose, contributing to anxiety, depression, and codependency. For years, there were countless women encountered, beautifully gifted and talented to reach incredible heights in and outside of their households. Some of these women applied the tools and resources suggested, achieving stability and progress. Others were beset by what people refer to as "generational curses", repeating negative cycles that directly impacted them and their children by way of the children's choices and behaviors in the home, school, and broader social environments. For decades now, issues like truancy, school fighting, growing gang involvement, and teenaged single parenthood have become so common that they are normalized. Numerous failed personal and familial relationships (burned bridges), as well as financial, mental, and emotional instabilities, have been among the various pervasive problems to solve.

It is long overdue for sounding the alarm. A beneficial women's empowerment program spends its time focused on the promotion of strategic programs that instill order and structure through educating, training, and coaching women on how to excel in their personal lives (building character and skills) that serve the home environment "first". This would entail these program leaders exemplifying and teaching other women about innate female functions and roles. There is no way around that. It should not center on catchy buzzwords such as "empowerment", "female leadership", "girl power/magic", and "boss chick", while ignoring the women that are paying and leaving these programs and conferences without substantial information and tools to improve their lives. Properly mentoring women requires compassion and honesty. Not one over the other. It is a necessity that any stable, seasoned woman be concerned about the livelihood of other developing women. Those who display love, and are genuinely concerned for other women, do not sit back and watch them drown from repeated obstructive choices. Love helps, teaches, and corrects. It does not promote famed, negative lifestyles that produce devastating outcomes for the average woman. From establishing a foundation of goodwill, with applied education and resources, women can flourish and present their wonderful trademarks, crucial to social functioning.

Embracing the womanhood journey requires courage. In efforts to revive or restore women, distractions must be eliminated. It is essential that social media "consumption" be monitored, and possibly reduced. As previously addressed, many of these entertainment sources seek to distract and amass profit from women's desire to receive attention and validation. Women are documented to spend more money than men, making them higher consumers. Think of the lucrative benefit to the retail, fashion, and music industries. Women are the center of their marketing strategies. In this epoch, everything and everyone is vying for women's attention and financial backing, depending on them to be a consistent "emotional consumer". A boundary must be established to "guard" the heart and mind from things and people that invoke strong emotions, luring time and energy away from fulfilling women's roles as a stable, productive, peace filled woman, daughter, granddaughter, niece, mother, or wife.

Daily choices determine the course of a woman's life, and of those attached to her. Referring back to the book of Genesis, spiritual believers are aware that Eve's wrong decision to continue conversation with her cunning Adversary, Satan, disguised in the form of a serpent, cost her and Adam their original relationship with God. Cutting off the "enticing conversation" would have eradicated the beguilement and resulting "fall" into sin (upon disobeying a clear God-given boundary). How many enticing conversations and situations are ladies involved in today that are destructive to their present and future lives? "Protection" comes with establishing and adhering to boundaries. Eve was the first woman to demonstrate how certain decisions can alter the course of lives. If she would have stayed under the covering (order and protection) of Adam, and Adam would have resisted her request by heeding the words of the Lord, they would not have been cast out of the Garden into the harshness of life's way. As the elder church women would say, "…but thank God for Jesus!". Adam and Eve's decision came with grave repercussions. Their decision to be deceived was forgiven, however, their choice still had to be atoned for. It was a selfish choice, as the good of the "collective" (future generations) was not reason enough to abstain from the temporal pleasure of what the serpent persuaded them to believe. So it is in present day, every adult decision produces outcomes, positive or negative, that can alter generations.

A "revival" is defined as an improvement in the condition or strength of something. To revive something is to make it notable and important again. The term is synonymous with making a comeback, resurrection, resuscitation, awakening, and rebirth. Possessing a holiness and apostolic spiritual background, I am all familiar with church revivals and the fact that you cannot have a "collective" revival without first having an "individual" one. Each individual must desire a change and betterment. In these spiritual revival experiences, I and many others, received the benefits of repentance (a change of heart and mind that alters life's course and choices), water baptism in the name of the Lord Jesus Christ (for the remission of sins, symbolic of being reborn), the infilling of the Holy Spirit (for daily guidance and a prayer language), and also the boundary of practicing sanctification (choosing to live and behave in a way that is set apart for God's special use and purpose). The choice to be revived spiritually is the same choice women have to revive their natural lives. In fact, women's spiritual and mental conditions often correlate with their natural life's condition. The gain from revival is so much greater than any losses. No one has to ask what women have lost (latched on like a ticking time bomb) to the gains of equal rights and opportunities. The moral and household economic losses are innumerable for the average woman's life.

Most of the time, a set order abates chaos. Creating a life of order and alignment, will stabilize choices. The definition of the term "formation" is the act of forming or process of being formed; it is also equated with the structure or arrangement of something. "Formation" is synonymous with the words: emergence, genesis, development, organization, creation, and shaping. The phrase, "Let's get in formation", should not be limited to a voguish catchphrase from a song. When heard, insight came, as the shaping, development, and organization of women's lives is of pertinence to a functional society. Women are often small children's first teachers, thus influencers of the next generations. The principal way for ladies to get in formation is by arranging their personal lives to produce valuable results, undiverted by undisciplined people and vain lifestyles. When women come into alignment, things and people around them begin to shift (often for the better), decreasing the chances of derailment.

Imagine the social results of women who establish, or continue to uphold standards, conveying respect, kindness, warmth, substance, and emotional and sexual discretion. Although the cultural climate looks bleak, it has never been a more necessary time to recover the special qualities of women. There is no demotion in becoming a feminine woman, rather a promotion. She exudes a noticeably distinct air from other females. As women leave the rat race mentality and come up for air, they can comfortably transition into their position of origin. With proper structures instated and healthy counsel received, women blossom into individuals who are not only needed, but cherished and honored. In a culture adrift, a healthy, loving, and traditional woman will always stand out. She is refreshed by her purpose. With undeniable evidence of these unique women's rise, the popular question will become, "Who's that lady?"

About the Author

Cavesha Fox Nero is an Alabama native. She was raised with humble, traditional roots as the second of five children to two loving parents. As a licensed social worker, she has served women and children in the areas of foster care, family preservation, and interstate child support enforcement since 2015. Facilitating resources for stability and proper care in families, is at her core. She attended and graduated from Columbia Southern University with a Master of Public Administration in 2016 and the University of South Alabama with a Bachelor of Social Work in 2013. Her pillars are faith and family. She enjoys spending quality time with her husband and son.

Also by Cavesha Fox Nero

The purpose for this book is to briefly examine key moments of the COVID pandemic that forced intense, life-altering decisions. It discusses how American citizens navigated murky waters, suffering and persevering amid setbacks and devastation. At the core, this book delves into the impact of mandated personal health decisions on the masses. It addresses how media messaging can work to bring harmony or conspire to create unproductive feuding. The question to ask is, "Were the measures solely instituted for the safety of the public or was this practice (a test run) for another agenda?". Motives must be unveiled for the American people to trust the plans implemented in the name of their health and well-being. It has been proven that mandates and coerced compliance accompany consequences with lasting impact.

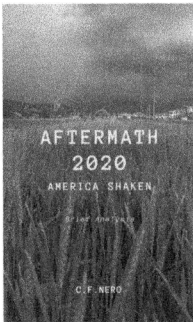

Aftermath 2020 America Shaken
This book is for the logical and curious mind desiring to explore all angles of the pandemic experience, with an open mind to variance of opinions.